IN THAILAND WITH THE APOSTLES

Joanna Sit

SPUYTEN DUYVIL
New York City

Thanks to Dante Alighieri, Ludovico Ariosto, Homer, Michele Madigan Somerville, Susan Montez. Without their work, this book would not exist.

My gratitude to the apostles: "Justice," "Farang," and "Baby Jesus." Equal gratitude to Peter Catapano, Bill Evans, David Kramer, Nava Renek, Thaddeus Rutkowski, Michael Sweeney, Tod Thilleman, and everyone in my family for their faith and support.

Library of Congress Cataloging-in-Publication Data

Sit, Joanna.
  [Poems. Selections]
  In Thailand With The Apostles / Joanna Sit.
    pages cm
  Poems.
  ISBN 978-0-923389-92-5
  I. Title.

PS3619.I83A6 2013

Notes

The poem is based on the idea of the *katuata*, a Japanese short form that asks a question as the first line and provides an answer at the end. The central idea is, according to Turco's *The Book of Forms*, that "the katuata answer is …intuited, as in the Zen koan or 'unanswerable question.' "

Terms

Dada: "Drugs" in Bahasa
Farang : "Foreigner" in Thai
Gamsahabmida: "Thank you" in Korean
Mekong: A river in Southeast Asia and the name
             of a whiskey in Thailand
Singha: Thailand's most popular beer
Wat: "Temple" in Thai

I. Flight

What dreams of grandeur,
do you think, make us fly?

We've heard there's a sinful city
across the world that bears no ill
will to virtue or vice, welcomes saints,

converts and conmen alike, that loves
the prodigal and the reckless and lights
the road for dopes bewildered

in ignorance and confusion. To see
for ourselves, we crawl inside
the belly of Korean Air, in this holy metal vessel

for one long flight into the tropics, glide over
slate blue June light, we go

to Thailand in search of the thousand joys. Me
and my two pals, Johnny Justice, Irish born
in Babylon, raised by the sea, and Farang,

privileged upper west side New York Jew,
and my beloved Baby Jesus, sprung from breath
of Christ and seasoned on Staten Island,

crusaders all, chasing love and glory

but not without senses of desire, duty,
fun, flying in this fat iron cross over
pastors, moors, to a temple near you. We ride

1

the clouds, smoke and drink, learn to thank people in Korean.
"Kam-sa-ha-mi-da...kamsa, karma..."

I'm chanting in my meditation, in my leopard
skin tights, dreaming my valium dreams,
far away from my friends,

from tungsten rainlight Somerville
to Miami moonlight Montez,
my midnight reruns, Otto repo cat,
Pudgy Skinless Chicken with Frank the social worker,

Already I miss them, I even long
sadly for my quarrelsome family.
Them too, I miss far into the stratosphere
to Seoul, where body lies dormant above the cumulus

while the cross careens East like a drunken
Baptist, expecting, crowned in smoke, air-
pocket fear...*thank you, kind stewardess
for the bloodymary, the red wine, white wine,*

Chivas even in coach. Kam-sa-ha-mi-da,
kamsaha...Jon Farang stretches himself, pale hair
pillows over the headrest offers from his stash.

"Perhaps another valium?"
Too late. Our communion invaded, walked-in on
by a host of noisy angels in uniforms and nametags,

"Bring me juices, pineapple, orange, anything
to avoid jetlag and constipation in the end."
First time traveler Johnny Justice, ADA,

Avenger of Corruption on Court Street Brooklyn, Lover
of All Women everywhere, charged by anticipation
and high hopes pops another pill.

I hum to myself and sip another water, light
another *Camel sin filter*. The wingtip bounces a little as it cuts through
flat white atmosphere. *Patty she likes rock-n-roll,*

a hot dog makes her lose control... we bring
our passion to the natives, we are. We're the glimpse
of salvation they're searching for. Johnny Justice is losing

his head over sweet Asian air hostess Amala. He's democratic
in matters of love and I wink at him. Lords of the open sky,
we are coming, tumbling, falling into mammoth

savage arms. Shafts of light curl on the edge of
rolling cirrus, emitting glory on the skin
of the cloud bed. In my convert awareness,

I declaim aloud, "that way to where the gods live!
That way to the prizes..." Daylight recedes. In rolls
the luscious sheet of darkness.

And behold! We are here,

we are coming.

II. One Night In Bangkok
Makes A Hard Man Crumble

To all dreamers who believe that
borne on wings all roads lead to paradise:

Not true.

Touching down I know already
if this isn't hell, it's at least
purgatory, for we are ready

to abandon some hope,
to slough through midnight
swelter where the wind sheds sweat

and plunge into the indoor hotel
pool Baby Jesus'd arranged from New York
weeks before. The wind feels

like a sirocco but there's no desert,
the wind tells me not to expect too
much, the wind tells me something will

go wrong. For the moment, we are
delirious with lack of sleep,
the flesh rotting heat flood

heavy on our eyes, stream between fingers
outside cab window. The wind tells me
all will be rewarded at the end.

Dark pagan city! I hear it moan, I hear
it weep, I hear its throat close around us.
The taxi deposits us in Chinatown,

the New Empire Hotel. In New York,
this would be the kind of pea green dive
Delmore could die in.

There is no pool,
no cool chlorine against this heat.
By narrow lanes and weak 4 am charcoal

light we walk without guide. Defeathered
chickens in piles on the cracked concrete
sidewalk edge, fruit vendors and mutilated

beggar shadows linger in the last darkness's
cul de sac, alleyways, gray stench everywhere,
where Farang gets hungry and wants to buy

an orange. The man behind the fruits ignores
us and turns his back. We point to the oranges,
and he turns to us, he wants 400 bahts for a fruit.

Outrageous! Farang cries, is offended

by his boorishness; we stand up to him
and stare back, point at the fruit like it's
the holy grail. The square Thai face turns to

us and in the dark, his eyes flare up like torches,
his jaw stretches wide and the pair of incisors
grow over his lower lips like a gate coming down.

Hair sprouts before our eyes and soon we see
nothing but those burning eyes and a long snout
curling over flesh tearing teeth and foam drip

from them like detergent. We don't know if it's
the surprise of the transformation or the low hungry
groan from his canine throat, but we shake our heads

now and give up on the fruit purchase. Before we can
find our Thai dictionary, he lowers his wolfish head
and lifts his haunches, poised to leap at us

and we jump away, knock into one another
and are almost pinned by the monster dog
before we run on through the coming light,

rotted ramparts of the dead and dying.
Towards daybreak, we find our way
back to New Empire and stop in the karaoke bar,
order Chinese tapas and beer. They fluster Farang

in the bathroom when he gets his shoulders rubbed
while pissing in the urinal. In this abyss
pop songs reek, excess burns through

the atmosphere. Stunned by jet-
lag, dehydration, deracination,
we take in the videos of dime-store trysts,

the bouncing ball over cheesy lyrics,
we edge closer to the realization:

> *We are here.*

Day for night, Bangkok stays
gray. Morning comes first in ominous
sound, distant rumblings of motors, then, forms.

Mercedes, Toyotas, Volvos, Fiats crawl
around traffic circles everywhere, tires screech
to jerky halts, bumper to bumper,
in tropical dense smog. On Yaowarat Road,

mad tuk-tuk drivers thread between lanes,
among blaring horns and striking sirens, the damned

wait entombed inside those tin boxes in slow
motion while the sun climbs closer to meridian.
And I watch from dim paint-peeling unwashed

window, see through the vapors the cursed
and furious faces that stare ahead. And I
look down in my jetlagged delirium, make out

the treacherous, the deceitful, the inconstant,
the eternally damned, bad dictators, ex-boyfriends,
men who raped their own mother

countries, rakes who violated women of all
kinds, each trapped in his airless vehicle —
I see Kurt Struver, defective lover extraordinaire,

chinless face shrunken by corruption, muddied
in sweat and dust, sandwiched between
General Chiang Kai-Shek's Rolls Royce

and General Franco's Mercedes rickshaw.
Serves you right, asshole, for taking advantage
of my youth, trying to shut me up with money and drugs

when all I asked for was your love and affection.

Trapped behind Baby Doc's Cadillac, I see
Pete Farlikas, drenched in exhaust fumes and choked
by the city's slime. True you were only 19

when I seduced you, but that's no excuse
for not loving me back after I compromise
my virtue and flaunt my disgrace

behind the trees that summer in Central Park,
when you married your pregnant girlfriend
with the bad perm and left the city without a word,

forsaking your destiny and memory of me
when you knew I was only asking for love and affection.
I gave you bums my shining moments, thinking you were

heroes, poets, kings, but you turned out to be maggots,
oozing sores, scourge, pestilence,
                  you can all go to hell.

I'm fished out of my reverie by the two Johnnies,
Farang, sun king among heretics, a people person,
plots to escape from grimy New Empire to

Ti-Ti Guest House; Justice, devotee of nature and pleasure palaces
sullened by dim air and cruel heat, squints
like a lost baptist in the leaden desert and assents.

Map in hand, the pilgrims step out onto mid-day
Bangkok streets, wrapped in polluted vapors
and industrial flame, pass hardware factories,

chicken wholesalers, radial vendors, men
in flip-flops squatting by their iron doors,
their wire fences. At the entrance

of an electrical store, a burnt shadow
hunched in the shade is none other
than my first inamorato, my childhood

sweetheart, Kwok Lum, prettier
than Einstein, brainier than Pat Boone;
I asked, "why'd you do it? Left me to the mercy

of that bitch your mother when I called you, why
in 20 years didn't you ever call me back?"
I wanted to recount the days of waiting,

8

my first feelings of love dried up, his silence
that followed me everywhere from subway
stations to the newly unionized sweatshop,

thinning out every sexy feeling before
it flowered, drying out every drop of romantic
moisture and stunting my growth.

"Why'd you do it? I could've been as gorgeous
as a hot house plum; instead, years I went
begging for love, fearing it, waiting for you,

dreams I had when I kept asking you
and waking up without your answer."
Now strangled by soot, unable to speak;

he gurgles and chokes, arms
waving in circles, the words he owes me
now vomited out and down his heat-desiccated

chest, some he swallows back
and regurgitates again as he is
racked by his own heaving cowardice.

Along the muddy river we plod
in our best safari-khaki high tech wear — none
more decked out than Farang, lover of blond

food and pale women, gold
and passport satcheled around his neck.
Our quartet, one Jew, two Christians, and me,

half mad Catholic, half baked Buddhist,
snake along the roads to motors amoan
and shell-shocked expectancy,

we arrive at the inn.

III.   Stomping at the Ti Ti

No sooner do we register our names
when Justice yearns to taste
the local reefer. Aside from Singha Beer,

seems that wild weeds don't grow
on trees as we were encouraged to think.
But as if God's looked down on this sorry

crew and is moved by Justice's trauma,
Farang meets Steve
Australian surfer pothead, condemned

by mysterious sin to live in Ti Ti's four walls
with one bed for his laundry, the other
his lost body. Through the cannabis haze

and ceiling fan hum, Surfer Steve sits and intones,
"It's a lifestyle choice" while everyone in the room
knows it's no choice at all. As the Buddhists say,

"every family has a mantra they can't chant."

And while Surfer Steve drones on,
the three apostles get too high and drift

toward distant shores in the windowless
room. Anxious to be rid of surfer philosophy,
piloted by induced claustrophobia we spin

from Ti-Ti's bleak walls and narrow beds
into a waiting tuk-tuk. Baby Jesus, Justice and I
sit on the narrow bench while Farang lies

on the tuk-tuk floor across our feet. Foot
to the pedal, our driver lowers his chin, looks
ahead and shoots off the curb. We slam onto

each other, riding the mad dragon
into oncoming night while bloodfilled
lights coast around us. In the rearview mirror,

the driver's mad eyes stare up at nothing
and we're sure this is our end. Near Kow San
Road, the tuk-tuk almost capsizes but rights

itself just in time to hit a bump
and we fly off our seats, knuckles white
from gripping of straps, shirts, knees.

I see ourselves splattered on the sidewalk,
mangled limbs, bloody passports and Amex
checks asunder, swirling in the moist

dark wind. I make mental amends to all those
I've wronged, gratitude to those who loved me:
Debra, sister, witness to the carnage

of childhood, whose love kept me enough
to keep living when I shouldn't. Goodbye
to my friends, who I will never again see.

The boys I've mistreated – Marc whose eye
I tried to stab with a sharpened Ticonderoga #3,
Leighton, prince among men, I did

you a grievous wrong when I spurned you
for an actor. Erica, my mentor and best
friend, whom I insulted, I loved you too much,

went too far. Jonathan Litter, because of my ego and vanity,
I lied to you 14 times when all you wanted
was to feel my lips, some of my love. I should've lay on your Columbia

dormitory bed and loved you
on that hung-over October afternoon,
but I was dishonest and wanted admiration.

Trapped in this speeding coffin,
clinging to the fringes of life
I reconsider while the stoic apostles remain

silent. I cry out. "I'll never
do it again! In the next life, I'll give plenty
to charity, I'll be true and virtuous if you let me

live…I am a corrupted soul, I sometimes make
fun of people and act superior and vindictive,
sometimes I try to get away with things,

mean acts, small pleasures. I haven't always
been honest, but I've mostly told the truth."

Inside this rattling death box, I become
my own confessor and forgive myself.

But we don't die. We disembark, like martinis,
stirred, shaken, but unbruised,

saved but not redeemed.

In the glowing pagan night, the river
flows towards Nirvana, where all things

are reshaped and returned to the web
of stars. Virtue has its rewards here
but not the kind we were taught

by rabbis or priests. Astray in this libertine metropolis
of river taxis and sex charged voices that murmur
through the neon, freefall through fusions

of despair and uncensored pleasure, beckoned
by saffron flutterings of boy monks
and secret heartbeats of Phat Pong whores,

we wander through the gurgling streets
blindfolded by strange tongues and a city's
chaos, lesser and lesser angels.

IV. Bizarre Bazaar

Shocked clean of illusions and expectations,
we continue another day unrecovered.
Among throngs of monks and other Thai

denizens, we bus towards the Weekend Market
on the other side of town, where the air seems
brighter and the Chow Prath River flows pass

slums and palaces alike. Guided by *Lonely Planet*
but aimless nevertheless,
into the mouth of the market

merely a maze of used jeans, rusty
crockery, polyester leisure wear organized
by stalls. Pressed to the tail of the crowd,

we shuffle chain gang style into the labyrinth,
turning not on our free choice but on the will
of the horde. The noonday heat funnels through

collective breath, hair, skin; the old
refugee fear wakes in me, and I reach out for
Baby Jesus, afraid to be separated, forever

lost from joy. We lose Farang as he takes
the first right turn and we are urged to
the left. By the stall of used bellbottom Wranglers,

I spot a familiar face I can't place. Anyway,
how would I know anyone in Bangkok?
The woman leans against the post,

her hairy face half hidden by the leg
of hanging Jordache. It's my childhood
friend Mary Farrugia, the Maltese bully from

Ludlow Street! Her hair, once tawny and full
of Mediterranean waves, now cropped
in prisoner fashion, is crushed under a double-knit

wool and mohair cap. Sweat drips over
her eyes as she squints up. "Mary," I say. "I thought you'd be
married by now, with beefy Maltese kids

and hairy Maltese husband. What're you doing
selling old jeans in a Thai flea market?
And what's up with this nasty outfit?"

I can hardly hear her answer as she sweats
and pants in the heat. "I've been sentenced
to endless suffering by slow flame. I can't take

off this double-sided alpaca cap unless my head goes off
with it. I'm boiling for eternity." She recounts
for me in whatever short breaths she can muster

how bullying and hypocrisy towards her friends
landed her in this torrid fate. It was true she
appropriated a $20 bill I found in the Essex

Street Market and made me buy her
a birthday cake instead of pizza when it wasn't
even her birthday. It was also true she took

advantage of my good nature and immigrant
naiveté when she convinced me she was better
for being white and treated me like shit. I want

to stay and hear her tale of woe, but the crowd
is restless and pushes me on, so I wave goodbye
to Mary, who, unshaved, unshowered, prays

as a good Catholic does, for spontaneous combustion.

Onward we snake past wails of such
condemned souls, moldy stench of the blighted

multitude stings our eyes, and tears well
up but no pity. Coming to a spice stall,
a shadow clamps against the wall, layers

of mohair and cashmere straitjacket almost
obscure the face of my lost friend Moody
Youngman. I lean over to touch him, to help

if I can, but am forced back by a sudden scorching
wind. He looks up and sees my face, in
his grimace, there's remorse, there's resignation

I've seen often in years past. Without asking, I know
his sin. He knows as I know, that he spurned me
by the orders of his jealous fiancée, who exiled me

from seven years of buddyhood, confessions
in the dark, left me to self-doubt, hurt me
in his silence. I don't care that I wasn't invited

to her bridal shower, but I blame him
for letting me go so easily. Even now,
he says nothing, caught in his complacence,

wired to the wall like a goat. I look away,
for even now I can't forget how I loved him,
even now, I remember the loneliness of the abandoned.

But I have new friends now, and they're with me,
and they'll never let me be orphaned by cowardly
husbands and rankled wives.

In the next stall, Justice,
Baby Jesus and I try on rayon batik pants

while Farang is swallowed further into
the catacomb of traitors. We move among
corrugated irons, pots, wilted plastic flowers
and 70s Angie Dickenson style jumpsuits

until by a slight turn, we rejoin Farang
and shuffle to the pit of the maze, where
animals are slaughtered and left to bleed

in the sun. Farang looks far away
to avoid the sight and Justice averts his eyes.
Yet, none can escape the piles of broken neck

chickens and skinned lambs strewn like flowers
in our path. Amidst this bloody cavity, a hand
shoots out from under a flayed calf

and grabs my ankle! I kick it away,
and with it, insects lift from the corpse like a veil.
Smeared by animal blood and dismembered

sheep, wrapped in woolen knits and acrylic
jumpsuits, legs pinned down by concrete ski-
boots, neck shackled by fox fur boa lies

Squidface Barbie, ultimate betrayer,
Machiavellian villain who bad-mouthed
me to Erica, called me a bitch, told her

to drop me, cut our affections, drove Erica
to a half a bottle of Stoli and accusations.
I was caught by surprise, I was shamed

into confessing things true and untrue.
She cries for help now, but no sound
nor sign can reach me. Blood

and sweat mat her hair and face on one side,
the other caked in maggots and worms. Her mouth

stuffed to the cheek in raw chicken necks
and ulcerated putrid livers, she looks up
in great torment. Yeah, like I fucking care,
low-life. I adored you, trusted you.

Instead, you damaged me, took away
my best friend and mentor. You taught me
about love and the movies, but at the end,

it was you who made me ashamed
of my half-formed self, my refugee privations.
It was you who renewed my pain of loss.

Are you sorry now? Or do you still enjoy
the taste of the ravaged?

Not a place of exoneration, we move further away

where animals are alive and running amok among
traumatized believers of sin and chaos. Beyond,
heat gathers density as we come upon the apex

of the afternoon. Half led by the animals,
we disgorge from the tail of the market
into the wet inert fire of the sinister capital.

V. High Noon

Unlike the market's moisture sodden rank
corpse sweat and dark animal fluids,
outside the deserted street stuns us

with the sun's livid lashing eye,
flaying our necks, fingers and lips, draining
out the streets' soot, blotting its tumescent

buildings. Disoriented first by what we see
in the heat bleached world, we wander
from street to street, parched and deflated

by this sudden hot silent light, this crackling afternoon.

As we march forward, natives watch us
ascend and descend the curves of glaring

roads, deem the two Johnnies and Baby
Jesus cheap horny Americans who're sharing
a Thai whore (who would be me). No use

protesting, I know. Never who I seem
to be, I have wandered continents in helpless
disguise. The good news: no more disguises needed,

no one cares here who I am, even if they're wrong.

Desperate for shade and small breeze,
Jon Farang, red scorched face noses
toward the river. Justice, Long Island nature boy,

is most unhappy caught in this urban discomfort.
He imagined icy umbrella cocktails on pliant veranda,
reclining on wicker and under palm, big feathered

fans maybe, but not dirty streets and poor
grubby populace, smogged traffic and grimy concrete.
We plod forward and kick up dust, the light

dry and suspended over us while the road
expands and contracts, then the trees start in
too, bend away and grow fat, then melt into

the glare, shrink into little brown rings that circle
around marble saplings, then reshape
to tiny orbs, dots and the whole world looks

like a Seurat gone mad, minute points scattered
over hot threads of white light, blood rises
and pills over spaces from somewhere eternal and

finally pools around our eyes. I barely see the road
in front and am sure some terrible episode will
do me in. I am determined not to faint, embarrass myself.

Baby J.'s soaked in sweat and missing his hand
I grip his shirttail instead. He pulls me along
aimless until a tender wash of light moves

near the river's edge, and a sad voice like
lost love breaks around me so that I can't
know its source. "No one in this world

has seen what I've seen, heard
what I've heard; the horde crying,
piteous broken things wrought

in war and peace. I've saved you once,
when you were barely a soul, I gave
you back life, rescued you from the realm

of the lame, the cripple, made you a gift
of song to use in compassion. I am your consecrated
mother, you my anointed gift." And there she is,

the Goddess of Mercy ahead of me, porcelain
skin and blue veins, smart face half veiled
from the pain infused air, eyes abrim

with human cries and suffering, her celestial
splendor soaks up the world. Her sad lips
plump from centuries of sorrow, she floats

towards us on her icy lotus. She's right, she saved
me once before, six months into the world
I was ravaged by polio though we didn't know
at the time. My mother, desperate, prayed to the Goddess

to save me and on a lonely road, put up a shrine
and forsworn beef for a lifetime and promised
my name to her. She's back to keep her vow

and save me once again. We're drowning birds
who grip the hem of her cool frothy Goddess gown,
and she pulls us up through the dust choked path to

a riverside bar shack tended by teenaged
butter skin Thai Rastafarians
who, seeing Americans and their Thai whore

put Bob Marley on the stereo and crack
open four bottles of Singha Beer. A fresh breeze
rolls over the stream and sways the skiff

at the pier's end, and Bob's voice rises over
the hut and pours down like rain, like ice, stretches
the flats and sharps gently around our skin,

and we pass from the saving hand of the Goddess
to float on the angel's voice. He sings "don't worry"
and we don't. I hunch over the round bar

table, vision still swarming with pulsing white
dots, the motion spills to the center of my nausea,
but the angel's song eases in again, the one beat

flows into the dim cool bar. Comforted at last,
we thank the gods for the grace of oasis, momentary
deliverance, and know that everything little thing is gonna be alright.

VI. A Day in the Country

Coined by Farang, de facto group jester
Val Kilmer look-alike, "what wat?" becomes
our incantation at times of boredom, filler between

phrases. To see the wats, we decide next morning
to go north, to Sukhothai, ancient city of temples
and enormous Buddhas. On leaving TT, Farang, lover

of Scandinavian non-colors, comes upon British
un-blonde Elizabeth, who can't hide her beauty in baggy
intern pants. The rest of us order vegetable omelettes

while Farang chats up the girl, only to find she's
leaving for the south. Regret and yearning in tow,
Farang and we board the train to the holy city,

departing from heartbreaking Bangkok to the bucolic realm
of grazing water buffaloes, huge Buddha
heads rising on mountaintops, singeing wood

from slash-and-burns. First time in days,
light rekindles in Justice's eyes, clear
breeze purging our third world urban narcosis.

At last, mantle of darkness lifted,
we are released into another type of wildness,
untamed light, jungle vines, rice patties, palmed

hamlets behind the trees, unconquerable country
no French nor Dutch nor British can claim or
colonize, mysterious zone of lawlessness

and cruelty no European can penetrate as
they have Burma, Vietnam, Malaysia. A blind
empire where thieves and beggars love the king.

Tired of Thai dives with holes on the shower floors
for toilets, we decide to go upscale at the Rajapruk
Hotel Guest House, cheap version of the Hotel

itself. Told we can use the hotel pool anyway,
it doesn't take long for us to don bathing suits and
order drinks poolside. As luck would have it,

Farang's heartbreak is assuaged by two Swedes
sunbathing topless next to us. Typical European
hubris defying native conventions of propriety.

Untutored in the magic of paradox
they flash body parts everywhere
They know they're in
Thailand, a country of limitless sex options and old-

fashioned modesty. But friendly Farang isn't
offended. He strolls over to make their
acquaintance, only to be politely but coolly received.

As we settle back in our deck chairs, a large black
cloud barrels over the vista and I hear the sound
of a collective sigh. I am filled

with mysterious terror and pity,
the air's humidity clings to me like a shroud.
Justice is just drying off. Baby J's still in

the pool. Farang reads the Tribune in shades;
the bare breasted Swedes murmur
to each other. All is well, and the dead are alive

all around us.

VII. Swamp Things

Outside our rooms lies the swamp,
a muddy pool of still water and rotted poles.
I knew at dinner this is a cursed

place when I found mosquito welts cluster
like grapes around my belly. The insects
come from the swamp, I know this as a sign like

a blood trail or stigmata. It always happens this way. There will be
visions and revelations, lights will go dim
and clouds will veil the moon.

At midnight, I wake and hear low moans
from the swamp. From my window, what I see
I watch with terror and glee. At first, vague

writhing forms against the poles. Then, a silver
cloud of mosquitoes wafts between the figures. Finally,
illuminated by sudden moonlight, I make out

the Nameless One, he who lured me, 8 years old,
up to his Broome Street 6th Floor apartment and
asked to see my tights. I backed out

through his door and ran so blindly down the stairs
that I ended in the basement, and hid there
listening to the sounds of his footsteps. Now, mosquitoes

cover his eyes, fly in and out of his nose
and ears; his tongue, so swollen from welts that
it hangs from his mouth, keeps his lips ajar.

The body behind him, run through by a pole
and hanging horizontally in midair, I recognize
too, one of my old molesters, Tony Farrugia,

brother to Mary, teenage miscreant and super
of my building. I knock on the window, too
spooked to go outside, hoping to catch his

eye, but soon realize those eyes are sealed
with boils while swarms encircle his groin
where the pole has drilled through. There,

the insects feast on the stale blood and
semen oozing from his wound. That's
too good for you, wretched felon,

who, as I walked in from school at 7pm,
met me with your flaccid dick hanging
out of your fly at the bottom of the stairs.

First night, I told myself "it's an accident"
and ignored you. Second night, I knew it
to be no accident. Third night, you pulled me

and pressed me against
that ghastly penis I almost choked,
scared me so I had to tell my mother,

who then sent my 7 and 6 year old brother
and sister to wait for me at the landing,

where brother got into a fight with sister
and pushed her down the stairs, where she
bit her tongue but didn't know it, and bled

all night into a tin basin until I called
the ambulance that took her to the hospital
where they sewed 17 stitches on her little tongue.

Go ahead, twitch away, scum knave!

Here, I'm interrupted by the swift leap
of a gecko across my vision, and for a moment,
the swamp is empty. I almost think I'm

dreaming until I see again the wretched
scene, anchored by mud and decades of sewage,
I recognize my great-grand uncle, Guayabera Wong,

ancient even when we were
young, immigrant fortune-cookie maker whose
left index and ring fingers and right index

and middle fingers went into the batter, as they
often did in those days. In those days, he let me
sit on his lap and asked me what I wanted to see.

I let him feel me up with fingerless hand
for an afternoon at the Music Palace, flank
steak and tomatoes at the Green Bamboo.

But you weren't satisfied, were you, bald
degenerate. You wanted to fuck me; yeah, like I was
going to do that for a movie and a $3.00 lunch.

You tried in front of my brothers and sister,
like it was a game they couldn't understand,
you left me no choice but to tell my mother;

a woman of tradition who respected her elders,
she banished you gently and never told you why.
Here you are, tied to a pole chest deep in dirt,

throat gnawed open, a concoction of blood and gristle
and sore encrusted skin hanging loose, mosquitoes
a black fist upon the wound. You flap your arms

so frantically, you use whatever fingers
you have to scratch the bites, but it's obvious
that you'll never have enough to bring reprieve.

Beside him floats Uncle Tom Ho, egg-shaped
half-deaf babysitter to Tim, who testing the waters,
patted a wet spot on my skirt and wanted to know

if my panties were wet too. Again, I told
my mother, but this time she wanted evidence
and hid in the closet. Confirmed, she took me,

12 years old, to the factory where I spent
the rest of my youth in sweatshop servitude
and humiliation. Grand Uncle Tom now floats

unhindered like a buoy on the gray water
as the swarm tats his body in swift and efficient
fashion. Unable to bear any more, I close

the shades. Beside me, Baby Jesus sleeps
without torment, but for how long? What strains
of sin will visit upon us, crush us with its

avenging hand? As daylight comes, I hear
the chants of Buddha over the fields, sweet
songs of mercy spread through the tangles

and woods while everywhere else, planes
crash, houses burn , ships sink, cars explode,
bridges collapse, bones shatter and no one is spared.

VIII.   Same Same But Different

Born under the sign of Capricorn, before and after
birth of Christ, both temperaments tick
through centuries of monoliths, deities,

wreckage, years done away and settled
in earth's crust; Farang and Baby Jesus came into
friendship from Ithaca to New York, kismet

forged in cold climates, both descended in winter
solstice '63, when the sea goat was constant
in Saturn. Days after Baby J. was born,

the earth stood still in the noon sky.
while the Holy Family huddled in the manger,
and the Magi walked across the sand,

converged in pyretic drive toward
that bright light. Seven days after
his birth, Farang, the other half, born too, to

release the world from its trance into motion,
to complete it, send it to spin again, the sun then
could be measured for its distances. This

was the transit that sent their stars towards
each other. The first and second coming
united, time gone and returned in a single pulse.

And here is the garden of Sukhothai, ruins
and mildewed Siddhartha, crumbling
clay images. Here the resting place of princely Gotama,

the regal one, the one who stayed under the banyan
and kept his mouth shut while the other, the son
of the carpenter, raged through Galilee

collecting devotion and promises of love.

Both born in the year of the Rabbit, one
Old Testament Jew raised by Christmas
trees and Christian songs, the other

Anno Domini, cradled in the center like the sun
by satellites of adoration, both spoiled by hunger
for immensity, both afflicted by dark moods

and burdens of rage, both haunted by sounds
of cosmic discontents. Here Baby
Jesus stands between clay feet fired by earth itself,

where the shrieks of the damaged and slaughtered
seep into rocks, slim world of historic love
above him, agonies we refuse to know but recognize

cling to him, spent incense ash parts
where he walks. Farang adrift
among shadows slanted in the orchard,

over silent crows and sharp coriander,
amber lights spread between lesions
in the stones, cold reminders of the infinite

disgust that cast them here, relics
of enormous love, mercy, abandoned,
corroded, eyes pried open still

to some bruised thing we handle like truth.
With our rented scooters we ride down tree-lined
lanes past ten storied Buddhas, through

bitter jasmine, Farang's hair haloed
by partial new moon this late day. Baby
Jesus sits on a foot of the giant Buddha,

and as Gemini crosses over the axis,
this pair stands quiet, both tend
by quick moving Venus to go from days

of melancholy to seconds of mirth, both
bend equally toward abysses and fueled
secret appetites, yet, Farang's in constant

spiral for light's purity, for the completeness
of refraction, photomerges all color into white,
ignites passion in glistening clarity,

and among soft bar lights, Chardonnay, Nordic
pale faced angels, he dove into the swell of
pearly breasts and swam between clear

filaments of mortality, often drunk on worship
and vodka, shunning creams and sauces,
sinning and redeeming himself all at once

while Baby Jesus soaks in dense tones, pigmentations,
eats grape leaves and blushing sausage, wraps himself
in cardamom, chilies, opaque thick curries bleeding into greens.

And the calm washes over this decrepit cloister
where redemption is no clashing army, blood
soaked icons, soldiers of Christ, but a litany

of stone. This is the world's confession left untended.

And if we die here? So what? Heaven or hell relived
in another body, the wheel spins. And in our next
life, they will still be friends, walking as they

are now, on a sea of sacred spoils, among
orchids, incense, and the light will wrap them
both in hymns, hosannas, hallelujahs, songs

that flood across millennia and rush the stars.

IX. Top North

Back from Sukhothai and on the move,
the apostles and I having no fixed destination
but go where we're called. To Farang's delight,

we meet Americans just back
from the north who describe the city
of Chang Mai, folded in Thai hills,

buttressed by woods and wats everywhere!
Emboldened by our recent religious experience
in Sukhothai, we move at the break of light

towards Top North. Is it Farang's dream
of heaven or the beneficence of saints
that we have come upon this Shangri-la

in the wilderness? To others, a second rate hotel
for junior level salesmen and housewife
trysts with b-grade swimming pool. For the apostles,

the pool atones for shabbiness while the café
adds the bonus of white meat chicken nuggets
and rice for Farang's ascetic tastes. We don't

know it yet, but we're at the mouth of apathy,
merely charging at random, our tracks a zigzag
across the map, hypotenuse across strange

fields. In the rain, we drift around town, rent
scooters, cash checks, buy local gongs, play
bongos with drunk Thai Rastafarians in a tour

bus, merge with the city's arterial blueprint, disappear

into a different wat everyday, Wednesday
Disney wat on a hilltop where golden stairs
lead to golden effigies and golden gates through

gold leaf trims, Thursday forest wat in the grove
among hibiscus and lemon grass; all the while,
lethargy seeps a little closer to the heart

until we wake to find ourselves wearing
T-shirts with cryptic messages that say
"the land of the temper, and you know,"

evidence religious ambience has done us
no good. We are neither wiser nor smarter but more
dazed and mystified, and when Justice

rings his new echoing gong in the morning,
Baby Jesus and I feel neither light nor salvation
but a dismal weight of dread that pushes us

away from the call of Justice and down
to the café where Farang is waiting
for the first batch of chicken nuggets and rice,

perusing maps for our next destination
and hatch plans to take off once more, to stay
focused, decide a path we can count on. Having

heard of the Golden Triangle and jungle treks
that end in weed wealth and glee, we point
our compass to the city of Fang, and while

the apostles go on a last tour of bars, I eat
at the café alone. By the trellised windows,
whitewashed balconies sectioned

in amethyst evening glow and night's
crimson dark clusters in corners and rooftops,
moves across distant hills over Buddha's

radiant head. The pool, this time of dusk,
is serene and muddy, warped by shifting light
from azalea pink to blood. I'm alone

in the tumbling dark while others watch
CNN in the dining room. I'm invisible
when the world is caught and sectioned

in wars, accidents, news where I'm not. I've been
fearing death in obscurity, but this? A funny way
to dissolve. From somewhere, someone's behind

me and I jump away like I've been shot,
I go from the shadows into lamplight. I retreat,
but not fast enough, a warm floral scent curls around

me and before I can turn, one claw's on my neck
and another grabs my wrist. We spin around like
two badly rehearsed dancers, and I can't

stop and give it the what for, I'm thrown
by the High Crotch and know I'm being wrestled.
At pool's edge, I shake clear to see a pair of white

patent leather mules, and I look up to my long time
enemy seducer, Erato, the crazy third muse of love poetry
who, steamed by my neglect of late, has come

for a final showdown. It's clear I can't crawl
away from this one. I lie still between her legs
until the patent mules turn to walk away and I sprang.

Giving her back what she dished out, I grip her neck
and hold her wrist. But no dancing this time.
I kick her leg out and while her Donna Summer

hair gets caught in my mouth, I toss her
on her back and in fine Fireman's Carry fashion fling
myself on her over-tanned midriff. I tighten my arm

around her neck and look into the face of beauty
gone bad, half crocked eyes dressed by Greta Garbo
false lashes. "Looks like you should've stop trying

years ago," I smell Shalimar as we
wait lip to lip in heavy breath; she doesn't
answer. Instead, she surprises me and squirms out

from under, rolls on my back, legs wrap around
my thigh and puts the Double Grape Vine to me.
I resist too late and she moves up and split

my legs apart. Now, I'm out of breath, alarmed
and wondering in my panic if I'll die here while everyone
else is watching death elsewhere. My creature bends

towards my ear and whispers, "do you think it's fun
for me, stuck with you, you lazy sack of shit?"
Her weight on me has reduced me to a whisper

and I answer. "Then leave me. I don't need you.
What've you done for me lately but give me fucking
writer's block, huh? I'm leaving you. I'm joining

Kundiman, I'll apply to Yaddo. They'll love me."
Surprised by my cruelty, she hesitates and almost
releases me, then thinks better of it. She says, "leave

them alone, you'll only disappoint." As she speaks,
I pull my hands from under and heave her up. For a point
I escape, "don't think you can pin me

that easy." I shake her off, turn behind her,
cup her left elbow with my left hand, press
my right on her belly and bend her forward.

I slide my leg between her leopard skin
pedal pushers and slip into the Split Scissors
while she's down. "If you can't write a good poem

with me, how do you think you can write with them?
They'll laugh you out of the biz." Undaunted,
she contracts and deflates under me, leaving me

to crash by the pool on my face. I'm barely standing
when my beast delivers the Flying Suplex, arms around
me, she pulls me ribs against ribs, pelvis against groin

and I groan from pain as my flesh sinks into hers. I worry

that if I abandon one muse, will the others
leave me too? The closed doors, eternal waiting

behind each one, a lifetime of torment awaits
like an open grave, like grief-stricken days,
the aloneness such that may be guaranteed

to me yawns in the distance, only…before
I have the chance to visualize this future,
she's flipped me above her head, and I graze

my mouth against her moussed and dry blown
hair, taste the musky tang of freesia. I fall
head first into the pool. The dented water. The loss

of breath. I splash and tread, but I see now
the plunge is deep. I swallow my humiliation
and furious shame, and swim against disgrace,

vast pearly rivers of the exile, along gray tombs,
dirty roads. Underwater, I can still hear that demon
yelling at me, her shrill curses muffled in the water and mixed

with tremors of earth's volcanoes and collected sighs
of failure. I float towards the gurgles of the defeated
and I hear doves cry for mercy. If I surrender,

let this current take me, I'll never come back, and this
loss is too easy to contemplate, this defeat too
simple to turn over in that afterlife when I'll be sitting

around somewhere doing nothing but. If I must, I need more
to count, to regret, to rail against, to curse the gods, I must
have another go at this, so I keep my head under water,

reverse my path, swim past seacaves of half-drowned
dabblers and dilettantes, strangled in sand and kelp.
I keep my heart

from beating less she hears me and like a convict
I slither back from the rim of oblivion to the hotel pool.
Unseen, I rise from the water and crawl around until I see

my ghoul filing her claws on a beach chair and taking in
the moon. I come behind while she whistles and whittles
unaware of my resurrection. I fling her up by the neck

over my shoulder, then forward again, slam her back
on the beach chair and break it. She's stunned,
tries to move, but like a turned over crab,

she can only flap and thrash. Up in air legs akimbo
like the Hulk, I slam myself across her belly,
and knock out her breath, limp under me, arms

clinging onto my neck like a contrite lover,
her venom is drained. She nods her defeat
and like the king after the revolution,

allows herself a last morsel of pride by keeping
her chin up as I pull her by the hair and shove
her into the pool, where she makes for the drain.

I stand alone now, the dark with me forever.
I am done.
Euterpe, Calliope, Polymnia, take her home!

Somewhere in the hills drift sounds
of karaoke and easy laughter, and from another
place, the soft moans

of a vanquished goddess drowning.

X. Farangs in Fang

From myths and legends of inscrutable Orientals
offering elixirs and potions for the weary of limbs,
low of spirits, weak of minds, we get this

idea Fang's the town for us. We figure it gateway
to heaven, figure it frontier wilderness,
figure it town of outlaws smoking fragrant

Thai hash, happy harvesters in crimson fields
of poppy, narcotic emporium for foreigners,
one side of the golden triangle, holy ghost

of intoxication nestled in the hills, phantasmagoric
vision and fanciful flights aplenty, and like prophets
we will eat strange berries, gorge on charmed herbs,

enraptured in visions of God, we'll see
our own true light. But first, we see Mr. Sing,
entertainer in dirty Guayabera and safari hat waiting

at the bus stop, where we disembark
dusty dirty full of envy for any man
who feels at home, even in this dung hole –

Mr. Sing sings Yankee Doodle Dandy, declares all
"good for democracy," we get the joke
and hypnotized, we follow him through

a town in construction and disarray — cross
over makeshift planks to his dilapidated guest
house where he shows us his photo album of satisfied

customers on week long jungle treks, and I
see Justice's yearning to cast himself
among fearless woodsy heroes in hiking Tevas

backpacked to the gullet with survival
gear, but we are poor pilgrims who can
afford a day trek to the hills, Sing says,

and while we wander out to this mosquito
infested one horse town for our evening
repast and nightly search for weed, we come

upon Fang Bar and think we hit eureka
when the Fang Bar brothers pull from their sleeves
the magic leaves that smell mysterious and sweet

like apples and flowers. The apostles strain towards
the offering and between hits we toast to Mr. Sing
with big shots of Mekong whiskey until smoke

gone, liquor gone, we shuffle among rubble,
lurch through gutted roads and disemboweled
streets in this freaky burg to Farang's rendition

of "you're a mean one, Mr. Sing." Next
morning, I feel like someone's clocked me
with a hammer as I reel to the third world

makeshift bathroom and gag when I brush
my teeth by the putrid toilet hole. Giving up
all hopes of comfort and renewal, dazed

and hung over, we arm ourselves with cigarettes
and milk candy from Fang General Store
for later offerings. Dry as sand, I ask Baby

Jesus to buy some water for the ride, but he tells us
we'll get some on the road. I'm doubtful but keep my
mouth shut, and with our two official Fang trek guides,

we motor from town to country, through
juniper shrubs and alfalfa, tick bushes and jungle
gerania, now and then, the smiling guides stop

their scooters to show us one or two spicy plants — but
not a drop of water. We're weak with Mekong whiskey
hangover, except Justice, who's stripped down

to Superman pecs, and with biceps dancing
in midday sun, he scampers like a muscular bunny
up the path after our guides, and is followed

by Baby J. while Farang walks with me.
All athirst and droughty, I make my slow ascent. Below,
quilted fields break into squares of sage, jade, teal,

peagreen and limegreen, U.S. $ green, olive and emerald,
verdant shades shimmer under fiery sun and flaming air,
and me and the apostles almost vanquished, inching

upwards, hugging hillside. Midway up, I hang
my head, retch on a thorny bush and sob
that I can't go on. Gentle Farang stands over me

and waits in the heat, his own face aflame
with what ails him. "Glory Be to God!" I say.
"I need water!" Farang reminds me that we haven't

any and we better go, catch up to the others. By now,
we see Justice above us, swift legs kicking up dust
as he nears hilltop. Baby Jesus is midway

between waiting for me on the gravelly road.
Finally, we all of us reach the top
of the hill, where a little village stands

in the shady glen, all sticks and bamboo
shelters, wooden slats for beds, dirt floors,
noonday flies rest on small dirty faces,

comfortable on baby cheeks, noses, lids
of eyes. These are unglamorous hill people. No
exotic woven hats and mystic colors, this. No

bright cloths and resplendent bangles in the wilderness
but tangled hair and brown mud rags. No sweet
song and ritual dancing but hungry stares and tired

shuffles along roadside. No robust rosy-cheeked Thai
angel but old woman bent at the waist smiling opium-black
teeth smile that put new terror in us and we back

away from her. "Come see the way they make rice,"
Fang Guide 1 says and we stand with the village crowd
while two men sift grain around a bamboo net

and a deranged pig runs in circles. "Now it's time
to give out the candy." Fang Guide 2 takes out his
handful of milky tootsie rolls and Marlboros

and all at once, we're surrounded by hands that grab
at us, hysterical fingers and voices come.
Disembodied. Demonic. Everywhere.

We're forced back along the road, but the crowd surges
forward as I shout and stamp. Farang raises
a warning hand and reminds me Thai etiquette forbids

the raising of voice. Burdened by hangover, thirst,
fatigue, I start to see that I have gone back,
that this is my home. I am

brought back to remember the details in case
I've forgotten what the sadness was, thrashing
about somewhere but always close, enough

that I can always touch it by drinking or crying.
Curse this low budget hillside trek, hill tribe people.
I've come so far just to see the familiar, life already

lived. Under a shaded tree, desperate Justice
takes a mouthful of local water when he remembers
and spits it on the ground. Everything made here

will make you sick. This late afternoon, we're
gagged by exhaustion, shame, and hang our heads
from the villagers, they who're hooked on America

like everyone else. Candy and cigarettes, sex
and penance. I may not look it, but I have cash aplenty
and live in Brooklyn, and I'm sorry we ever came

to this pathetic dump where we wouldn't dream
to spend the night. Now, poverty too, a tourist
attraction, and drenched in cosmic guilt enough

to make a girl renounce all earthly pleasures, yet not
enough to clean the stink of money from our hands,
nor wash the reeking hubris off our skin,

we flee the village with Guides 1 and 2, turn from
the grim light of July and cosmic wrath
toward the teeth of fast coming darkness, no longer golden.

XI.   Half Truth, Half Justice

I see him moving, in his troubled
journey from the start, tough clam
born on the shores of Babylon, L. I.,

under twin stars : one for love, one
for bitterness, he too split down the middle
most times turning on the world with one

or the other, a foot in the luscious seraglio
of Venus, wet in the surf, the other bolted
tight to punishing rocks, spawned between

the Law's furious hand and Love's tender arm,
he's followed one then the other, at times the two
mingle, but mostly the law keeps the sword

in his hand, keeps him deeper in that brine
of tradition, so pickled for that
tongue curdling, spine-tingling lust,

for justice more than truth, where the way is paved
with red for blood, white for race, blue for uniform,
cruel and true as Superman, Johnny Justice, ex-wrestler,

self-made Lothario, Brooklyn Prosecuting District Attorney
moves between sky and earth, then wanting something too,
here in this un-American country, he seeks experience,

knowledge, but mostly pleasure – of flesh, of mind,
unlike Farang, Justice loves the country but its natives
he's got no use for and his shyness hides disdain.

He sometimes passes for gentle but we know
better, that though he looks like St. Francis doesn't
mean he is, that beneath his tourist tees moves

a torso ridged by years of weights lifted
out of faith for self-made destiny.
When man pits his body against nature,

man will win or die, and I see that myth moving
along the riverside veranda of Maekok River Lodge,
the perfect fancy pleasure palace Justice likes.

I see him moving, unbelieving and faithful between
the world and us, rigid in his muscles,
loving his friends, distrusting all others,

one side moves towards us, the other barring all
entry from strangers, trespassers who might wander
by accident into that touchy zone where he keeps

all fear. I see him moving, small American among
the Thais, true believer of Christ and retribution,
untouched by the natives conceived in Zen,

shocked by the unruly lawless land itself,
intimidated by a nature he can't beat by climbing it,
riding it, or sliding it. I see him, this man of law

moving through the jungle, not quite lost
not quite found, suspended in his need
for the soft lap of luxury and regard for the steel

toe of the jackboot, moving cautious, silent
about weakness, secretive about fear, he walks
on his toes in the animal preserve,

too afraid to disturb his own relief at being
here, among frangipani, gardenia,
like his pleasure might then be invisible

to the eyes of the peacock, to the scent-quick
baboons. And he doesn't notice me half asleep
on the veranda beside the river, and that I see

him moving under the banana leaves, for now one
with himself and his enemy nature, at this small
moment, the tough guy gives up a little of his swagger.

XII. Crossing

Clay Buddha behind the sun, enormous head rises through the
trees, inside the jungle he sits with palms up, one overlapping the
other but we can only imagine from where we stand, on the edge of
the river waiting for the long tail boat.

There're times when even tourists are smitten with insight, when
the sun-bleached air hangs dead on our heads and the water charges
blind hungry through earth, we're forced to turn our eyes to some
crumbling walls forgotten since who knows when, look into our
own creepy landscape with a late knowledge that we're strangers
to ourselves, and could be we've lost our compass.

The apostles sit line straight in the bamboo gazebo, a trinity of soft
stale doubt and certainty, weirdly connecting and keeping them
still when the boatman in a baseball cap drifts into sight, and the
minutes turn sluggish when he leans on the motor and slows the
vessel.

We all read the word "BOY" on the ferryman's cap. Head to toe
sardine-style we get packed across the vessel, human backs against
boat sides, me between the feet of Baby Jesus and Farang we depart
from the shore of Takthon.

The river runs swift and mean like a fever as Boy the boatman grins
the mad Thai grin,
races the motor between rocks and boulders over the river, knocking
out introspection
and reverie, one way and another giving us the repeat treatment of
the mad tuk-tuk ride so long ago. We are travel-dumb and can only
sit silent filled with unsung sutras and I get the spooky feeling I'm
leaving behind something, a book, a sock, cotton panties, an opera
of my life.

Boy guns his motor again, pulling through watery crags,
each looking more like a tombstone by the second while the
weather crosses the day with sameness of sun, dry speckled
heat, dust kicked up by general torment lying about the marsh.

Midway, Boy flexes his brown arms and stops the boat. We
come on shore to chained elephants ride-rentable but we don't
ask the price. Farang is instantly surrounded by a bevy of short
women in faded tribal dress, and his blondness glimmers like a
yellow stigma in the dark flower.

They stretch towards him and offer beads and bangles, one
or two dangling kiffs in their mouths. Meanwhile, we stand
on the shore side heavy with chained elephants and tribal
markets, no room to be lost amidst the garland of women come
to us like dust to broom every time we move. Justice reaches
out and Farang bends

to look at the rings, but what they offer up
is no bangle nor bead but letters, envelopes float
in static air and drop at our feet, words

of confession, desire, regret, blame, some
browned with years of waiting,
others crumpled by nervous hands. We realize

these are messages to the dead, notes to those
lost to sin, madness, folly, error, time's corruption.

The last words never read.

The apostles move back toward
the boat. I move among the lowing women,
dodging the dead letter that may be meant

for me. Each of us knows in our own
way we're unworthy of this task, it
demands purity we don't yet have.

Justice is first to get away and reach
the boat and seems glad to be free
from the shore. And as mad Boy pushes us

away onto the river, we hear faint cries
of captive elephants among the orchids,
I see an old lady waving a letter on shore,

and I think I hear her say against that hard sheet
of heat and roaring wall of the motor,
"it's getting harder every moment. But don't

worry, it's not too late to be ashamed."
Behind us, another load of Europeans dislodge
from the long tail boat all young and bleached

of irony, and I take her word for it. One of them
will do what we didn't do. At some moment, we will
have enough courage to give everyone another chance.

XIII. Americans Embarrassed

I'm trying to put a distance between me
and the prickly habits of denying repentance.
Remorse is the only thing I know how to get rid of,

and back in the States, I would've suppressed
the daily onslaught of guilt's sour taste
and dissatisfaction with a facial, a costly

application of oils and balms, silks and linen.
Here, nothing to do but sludge through the days
and let time shift and culture shock until we're

numb with boredom of the new, and in that
state, we unknowing enter the zone of the conceit,

a calm metropolis, a cloudy town
with no obvious villainy. No promise of sybaritic
pleasures Justice needs but plain streets

and common shops selling common things.
It's time to split up, us four, so Baby and I
stay at the thatch-roofed Sala-Thai

while Justice and Farang run for the big
hotel complex across town. The rain comes
down toward evening, and we're holed up

without contact. I read a sad story
while Baby jams with our teenage rock-n-
rolling concierges in bell bottom Wranglers

and paisley shirts. We're veiled in some shade
of indolence. The rain keeps everything in rot,
and the rottenness of this strange land is climbing

on us. We wander through town hypnotized
by our own secret narrative, guided by one
another's indifference, we've lost our drive,

we feel nothing but dull wrath. Sameness presses down
and we sleepwalk to restaurants at night, drink
Singha and eat hot noodles and rice. Farang rejects

us for comfort in others while we three're left
to huddle closer and stare out at a city of
smoking men and barefoot children – if this is

the third world, where's the first world?
the second? Is this a world at all? And where
does it go? Muddy pointless questions sink

heavy around us and chains us to our irritation.
This air breeds contempt in all its tourists,
and we're hit with a blast of hostility to plants

and clay, polyester and concrete, loathing
fills up our lungs and overtakes us
with petulance. Under this spell,

Farang's quick depressions now manifest
and his disdain for us twists sharp as glass
as he walks ahead. He wants others – such

that he's never known before. He worships
the neoteric Caucasian who shares this moment
of orbit and territory. He laughs at their jokes,

hangs on their views, but he's testy with us
his poor relations, shameless, we hang on,
a ragged family who mortifies

with our parched skin and dumpy clothes,
stinking of the boroughs and the East River.
But Farang's not the only one poisoned

by this city's serpent. Breeding in Justice
is another distaste for the people of the land,
he's annoyed at their lack of appreciation

for domestic progress and efficient plumbing,
their ignorance of English and proper comfort,

prouder each minute that he's American.

All of us afflicted with pride and irrational
homesickness, we've been bitten by some
faithless viper, and we're all itching

in discontent. Demented in our separate
ignorance, we sit at the town eatery and wait.
We wait for the familiar, the cure of all ills:

American breakfast: coffee, eggs and bacon.

Some Asian blend or regular American
Maxwell House? Folgers? Chock Full of Nuts?

Justice's juice is filled with ice,
and we won't have it – what with their shady
water system and backward culture. We may

be contaminated, defiled, polluted. The pale
boy waiter, so eager to please, hops right
over but doesn't understand American

Justice, keeps smiling and holding the glass
of juice and nodding his head. He'd do
anything for us if only he knew what it was.

He slips away, bowing and smiling,
returns with another orange juice with ice.
Justice exasperated, sneers

snaps "no ice." The boy's face keeps the distressed
suffering look of the eternally
indentured, and he looks to me at last

for translation. I shrug and we point to the glass
and for a moment, fear quivers in his eyes
while other diners look our way. I'm now

contrite and abashed, even when the coffee turns
out to be Nescafe, we have no more hubris to throw
around attitude. We drink in disgrace and eat in shame

in our own grim decrepitude wanting nothing
but to get the hell out of this burg. We stagger
out under thick mean clouds, gray streets

busy with rubber thonged feet and ragged sarongs,
wild children wave and call out to us. "Hello, Joe!"
They stand rod straight when they do that,

little dirty soldiers or refugees eager
to please, like that boy in the restaurant
eager to please, everyone eager to please

us while we fester with pride. They want
our lives, but who doesn't? Just think
of the riches they imagine we have –

movie stars, roulette wheels, porcelain bathtubs –
what they must fantasize while squatting
over the shithole. How could they know

they've stripped us, their innocent adoration
wipes clean our vanity and conceit. We move
among their outstretched hands like paper

saints in a city hazy with new sun, and as we pass
along its walls, veiled copper by incense smoke
and moist air, the children's laughter glides

over us and wraps us in some dream of joy.
We don't know how to leave, we don't know the way
from this sloth that makes us too satisfied but not

happy enough for peace. So we wait in the Reggae Bar
like waiting for a train that never comes.
We smile at the little prostitute behind the bar,

but not too closely, and we wait.

XIV. Shattered

The prostitute giggles behind the Reggae Bar
when sensing our angst and shame, eager to save us
from ourselves she points us back up north to Mai Sai,

willing to go herself and keep the apostles company
until she gets the sense they aren't buying.
She gets the faint whiff of virtue but no

carnal yearning among the three. So we go, fighting
heavy currents of apathy and frayed camaraderie, bus
to the green hillside border town connecting Burma

by a bridge and walk the dirt road to Ya House,
for sure, Farang and Justice think, this is the stop
to paradise, and like the sign on the wooden gate says,

"everything possible." We know this to be
a celestial heart pouring out all that we need
to make us good again, a grassy glade lined

by a row of cabins, entire complex roped off
by a river. We're already imagining ourselves
on the reception pavilion terrace looking towards

the river, smoking potent Thai hash and wandering
along the one road that leads out of town, we
would follow the laughing half-clad children

and half-mad mongrels, we would learn to love
each other again and prance among stained poppies
and holy weed like evangelists. There is hope

in this town for us, much else we can't tell.
Like always, motion carried on unseen promises,
we enter the morning city on rented scooters

and we separate at the mouth of town
like tossed grains of sand and scatter ourselves
in all directions, Farang heads for the border

and Justice hangs around saucy local
women in silk sarongs. Baby Jesus
and I dine on noodles and shop for batik

like faithful tourists, but just when we're
filled with curry dumplings and a warm sense
that all's good with the world, we come across

a crumbly bridge over a veiny brook
snaking to the Miliusa trees. Town
noise flows and stops, a curtain raises then drops

on the road we've just crossed. In front
of us even the air is compressed with silence
until we walk into it. Then, cries of thousands

press on us and shackle us to our spot
and all around us, fetuses of all sizes lie
on the grass and half buried in the muddy bank, some

still attached to torn umbilicals
dipped in the water, some tangled
by their cords, bloody blue limbs flail and some

shaken with cold, some without limbs yet,
half tadpole, half human lie on their sides
unable to move, the earth covered by uterine

mucus and crushed placenta, aborted lives
sliding here and there mostly cold
and like clay dropped into this

world neither here nor there. I stand
among the embryos afraid to walk lest
I step on some, but finally I move

because I suddenly remember a baby
I once knew, or would have known
if not for poverty. We tiptoe with care

and at times the little bits of flesh
on the ground slide under our feet. Not
knowing what to look for, I have

no doubt I'll know it when I see it.
It's been so long, years full of silence
and amnesia about that day when I stood

by the hospital window on Grosvenor Square
and waited for the doctor. In the strange
white room, folded neat and straight under

the starched white sheets, she looked up
and asked if the doctor had put it in a jar,
and if he did, could she see it? I didn't know

what "it" was, but I translated anyway.
She wanted to keep the jar if she could.
The doctor said no, there was no jar.

She wept a little. And the next day,
in algebra, I drew eyes around the unknown
X, the factor proving that all its conditions

indeed exist. But I still didn't know
what it was I was called to do that day,
not for years, not in anyone's memory

but mine. And here the fertile ground
for shortened lives, not even a place
of honor for the righteous dead

but a mere patch of rotten earth
where they lie unburied. Here are ones
who were still in gallon-sized plastic bags,

motel towels folding them in,
those who've arrived here by accidents
of cars, fallen trees, hurricanes, those

who haven't taken their first breath
and those who've taken a taste of it
and then deprived of it,

those half-formed ones who lost their own
bearings and slipped from the womb,
the accidental letting go, the miscarried.

I circle the embryos and protoplasm,
the blue skin and gray flesh, abandoned
to earth like clay untouched

and while wondering about their souls
I come upon a gray mass of tissue
under a banyan by the stream. A sudden

flush of heat shoots through me
and I'm paralyzed by this zygote
vibrating with doom. This is the one

my mother kept so briefly, the last
one no one knows or remembers
lying by the water for eternity

without a past, a gender, waiting
for me, the sister it never had.
Don't ask me how I know,

there're some things
we're all born to recognize
and inside these shallow woods

the innocent are weeping like songs, voices
shake the saplings, pull the rivulet,
those with arms reach up from silt

and dirt, skinny arms and legs shake and wave,
milky eyelids close over promises of life.
In this bloody nursery we're all drowning

in the hymns of the pure, dark sleep
before Eden, before pain and separation,
before sin, and here begins the end

of the mean world, transgression redeemed
in a zone of purity, and we stand innocent
in love, me and Baby Jesus, clean in their tears.

XV.   Everybody Knows This Is Nowhere

We've now reached the top of the world,
the mountains, clouds and sky close
then open to us, sharp gleams of the river

for a day deflect our sickness for comfort
and home. What with occasional bickering,
negotiating for food and drink we

believe now that we are where we belong,
except we sense the lack as we play
cards into the night, drunk on Mekong up

in the hills, river flowing behind the cabins,
we feel the chill of useless drifting in
and out of towns, wats, palaces, huts, humors,

noodle shops. We're transfixed by this aimless
wandering, the looking and going through
places, numbed by the same lessons in sin.

We're up here among pink orchids and
hibiscus, banyans and ferns, but so far away
from home or heaven. Paradise is somewhere

else we can get to by plane, train, boat, and by
next day we're on a rusty bus passing palatial
huts and cool verandas – one day I'll be back

on this edge of existence and coconut palms,
I'll wear sarongs all day, sit in the shaded
terrace, drink watermelon juice and drive

a Mercedes Benz. But now, I'm worn out
by all the condemned, the ruptured, and want
nothing but cloister, separation, silence.

In the meantime, we are heading south
pressing on to the beach even if it means
we must retrace our recent steps through

Chang Rai and Bangkok. Justice leans against
the dirty window and dozes, having enough
of water buffalos and local farm life while

Farang, tethered like livestock to his money satchel,
adjusts the cord around his neck. By the time we get
to Chang Rai and check into Sukranrat Hotel,

dense boredom's eaten into flesh and bone
so Farang, pulling on his money satchel
buys us passage on the first plane out

and first light of day we take off and say good-
bye to the north, watch from the plane window
the slow receding grass line of the foothills,

the lazy wooden barge floating dreamy
on the river shallows, half hidden in palm
fronds and meadow plants, the Maekok

River wearing down mildewed stones.
Justice, folded into his seat by illness
stares out stone faced and stoic while we cut

over wild uplands towards the sea.

From one edge of earth to another, we touch
down on Bangkok once again, this time we know
what to do and go directly to Kao San Road,

home to all backpacking, sandal wearing rejects
of the western world. I move with a plague
of assorted insects crawling beneath my skin,

quarter-size welts eat into my belly and arms,
sharp itch chills me to my spine
while *The Terminator* flickers on the video in Buddy's

Guest House bar. I smoke and drink and try
to forget and almost do when we finally
leave Bangkok's bedbug infested rooms,

duck the cold eggs and slimy banana
breakfast on the overnight train, and by
the bleak morning light, we're heading

to the pier in an air conditioned bus and feel
the sea coming near, we look to the lush
warm waves, the salty tingle, and all better,

we disembark onto the marina. But as if hell
had not finished with us yet – or maybe heaven's
just beginning to take note, Farang looks for his

money for a cup of coffee and finds everything lost.

The satchel that gave him so much trouble
and doubt has finally disengaged from his neck
on the bus. How he doesn't remember, where

he can't recall. It's a victimless crime – is it
a crime at all? Could be no one's to blame
when Farang himself can't get attached

to his own possession. The search begins and ends
on the bus, but like we expect, nothing is
recovered and we're forced to get on the ship

and continue onward. Asea, Farang stands beside me
and we look out over foggy horizon. A lone
dory drifts close and crawls along the sea line.

Farang too, stripped of passport, name, money,
drifts without word towards a brand new place
we can't know. *Man, I'd like a massage about now,*

I said to the sea. And everybody knows he can use a joint.
He has no choice but to ground it out
sure that this will bring him closer to some

grander state, or to some gothic future
of "I lost it all in Thailand and now I'm beggin'
for a living in the hot sun of Surai Thani."

What's real finally is not the loss but the test
of virtue, the chosen recipient of the plague
who's closest to the heart of God. This is the end

of nowhere and he alone is safe among us.

XVI. Strangers in Paradise

Because we insist, here's the clear blue sky.
Because we persist, here's the white sand beach.
Because we exist, here's the gate of paradise

open the moment we touch down early
afternoon, curvy bikini-girls in great flocks
with milky coconut drinks lolly in the surf

and the whole thing looks at first
like Club Med and we're glad to be
here under the sun like this, where

even Farang, fresh from dispossession,
smiles at the blond Australian girl brushing
by, and Justice directly heads for the water.

Baby Jesus and I stay on JR Bungalows'
café veranda and order Thai omelettes, cold
beer, and we're sure that here's the place

to heal us from all uncertainty, tension
of the unknown, because here we know
everything. We know the clean light of day

and salty taste of sea, we know the tang
of pineapples, the sweet of coconuts, and the cool
shade of palm fronds midafternoon, we see

the romance, the fantasy and we know it
was invented for all farangs everywhere
as long as you're from the First World.
Here, all waiters know how to say "thank you,"

and no one will give you ice in your Pina
Colada without your permission, just another

part of the world submitted to our pleasure,
where Thai girls sell nautical print sarongs
and braid the glistening hair of western

goddesses, oil them creamy for their stay.
They'll corn row your hair and rub you
down and the price is always right.

And like gods descended from Olympus,
we glow in the sand and heavy sun, wheel around
dirt roads and up island mountains on motor

bikes, me behind Baby Jesus where we
sometimes wipe out at steep dirt hills
and lose our postcards, pens dropping

from our pockets, but Baby, he never complains.
We fly through the calm of this fair weather
along rocky coast through uplands, island

natives standing outside their shack watching,
some wave, others stare as if thinking
how cheap three men must be to hire

one prostitute among them. And sudden
moments, the itch of prickly heat reminds
me of my own foreign state where I don't

belong even to the gang of tourists, that
I'm not one of them, whoever they are.
But the sea gleams too bright in the topaz

sky for me to care and we're all glassy
with American needs, all stained by the sun.
Days we soak on beach chairs, half in half
out in the Gulf of Siam, warm bubbles swirl

and break against our thighs while we drink
Singha and Farang flirts with Australians everywhere.

When the sun lets go in evening, we walk on
sand, eat tortellini, pizza, noodles
and Singha, let mosquitoes eat us. Late

at night, the apostles dance half naked
in the Green Mango island discotheque,
where genders merge one way or the other,

and the lights never give anything away. Here's
the place we dream of, here's the zone
we were meant to be in. Here Justice loses his

pout because he respects the sea. Here's where
Farang forgets his hardship, drinks sangria
on credit while holding hands with Melinda

the Australian nose ringed girl. Here's where everyone's
forgiven and ignored for all sins, real or imagined, cruel
or kind. Here there's no tree of knowledge, but many

herbs of oblivion. Here, no one wants the apple, we
have mangoes. From here, we see Olympus
cloudy and high between Sirius and Columba,

we see the breasts of Athena rise over Antares,
the hem of Kuan Yin on the edge of Hydra. Here we
lose our habits, our memory, our handcuffs, our vows,

cut our losses, hide our conscience. Here we disappear
into our appetites, our navels, contemplate the days before
we were born. No one cares
what we do because God's not here.

XVII. The Faun in the Bulldog

Although God's absent and paradise's unwatched, Justice
is always on duty. Captive in American honor and self-
made pride, he's not without compassion for the less

fortunate and the oppressed even as he loses himself
to the hot lights of the third world resort; softened by
the island's savage nature, he's ready to save the beauty

from the beast. Two days in surf and sun, we seek
shelter from the blinding day in the Australian Bull-
dog Tavern. Singhas in hand, we come face to face

with the goddess behind the bar. At first glance,
we're struck silly like victims of lightening or deaf
men who hear a sudden burst of Tosca, cherubim

and lights spin for miles around and we're sure
we've just been blessed by a leftover miracle,
a lost moon just discovered, in this dinghy dive,

we are struck dumb, struck blind, while the angels
burst into hosannas, and Helen of Troy weeps ashamed

because this girl is made from the Divine Spirit and left
in Paradise to dazzle the snake.

Because she is filled with God's wrath and Buddha's
joy and looks out with dark keen eyes into sins of
the world and the uncertain nature of Justice without blame.

Because God has made her pure and Buddha's given
her serenity and she lives in evil and darkness
and asks for money with her immaculate body.

Because she is living proof of something created and then uncreated.

Because her hair is long and straight and black
and when she flings it around gives off the scent
of the sweet taste of the sick soul.

Because a sacred light radiates through her creamy and olive
and spotless skin and makes you believe that all you need
to be happy is love and a drink.

Because she is young and already knows the lusts
and cruelty of all men in this world and may take
advantage of this if they let her.

Because she is appetite in motion for anyone
who looks at her even as she moves away.

Because she is unlearned and greedy and knows
the value of a baht and a dollar and a franc and a deutschmark and a yen.

Because she is loved and unloved, had and abandoned,
asks with her hot house eyes, her velvet throat,
"can you buy me?" and "for how long?"

Because she dances alone to the Rolling Stones
and laughs at the other two bargirls' secret jokes
with sidelong looks of melancholy.

Because the gods gave her grace
gave her destiny and left her alone to glow in the blaze
of her own wild beauty.

Because alone she grew out of dirt and mud
like a lotus flaming from the water.

Because she is a bird of paradise.

Because God put a price on her and Buddha took it
away that now she's worth all and nothing.

Because she is bashful and blushes when she swings
her bare leg over the moped seat and gives a hint
of smut with a look of love.

Because she asks without asking for men's blind
desire and promises loathing and pleasure.

Because she's cast her charms on Justice
and he's touched by her fate and gets the idea
of Superman to the rescue.

No divinity left here but Justice, he proposes
that we take her to New York and she smiles
and says yes, she has a passport and loves America.

But her joy cut short as he accounts for her
the happy life she'd have once she learns
to type and he'd find her an apartment

where she'd spend her days as clerk or
secretary and like Lois Lane live free
of whoredom but enslaved to ambition.

Justice's vision of a life unstained comes
thundering to us, and just as fast her eyes cloud
over with certainty of another kind of servitude

and misery. She tells him she would miss
her family, and the U.S. is too far away,
and Justice is crushed. He's hoping for

a happy ending, a scene before the movie
fades where the swain saves the damsel in distress
and the prince is in the castle with Snow White.

Except: the princess never takes dictation
and the hero always pays, that there's no
difference in filing and fellatio, except one

takes longer. Eight beers later, we stumble
onto the beach, where the sea's turned dark
against the fading day. Lights and music drift

from The Island bungalows where Farang, not
looking to save anyone but himself, Marlboro
Light and sangria in hand, dallies with his new

crowd, Melinda to his left, Paul to his right,
drinking on credit and idle thoughts of romance.
Justice and I walk away from that scene

toward the water, gloomy in our failure to save
the fawn from the Bulldog. While fireflies glimmer
against a gray evening, wind from the East

uncoils and stirs inside the loosening heat.
Buddha chuckles kindly in the breeze, faint hands
break the moonlight on the surf, invite us

to see what our pity is, know that it's his
hands dancing like moonlight on the sea, know that
it's empty, useless, this pity that stays the darkness

that we're chained down to and lost in. The music
rises up along the beach, the scent of burnt jungle
creeps to the edge, where we're alone and waiting.

XVIII. Justice Pursued

Deflated by innocent whores and missing
his girl back home, what can a poor boy do?
Justice walks out on the beach and strolls

towards The Island where Farang and his train
are leaning back on their wicker chairs on
the veranda, pass Anita still massaging fat

hairy Antonio, who snorts piglike and digs
his big toe in the sand. Justice needs a big
drink, preferably Jamison but knows he'll have

to settle for Singha or sangria. Under thatched
roofs some girls are humming some low ditty
he can't understand. This girl will braid your hair

for a song. That girl will rub you until you squeal
like a born again miscreant. But all he wants is to save
the faun girl, give her an American Dream to sleep by

because she's too beautiful to whore in
that seedy dive. Why can't she see that it's better
to work for her money? Too late, now all he wants

is to forget he tried. High minded and humbled,
it's time to get in on the action. This is how
he comes to the Green Mango with Farang and his crowd.

So while I am puffing powder on my prickly heat
knees and Baby Jesus reads the guide book,
the two apostles lose themselves in the klieg light

heat, amid thin twisting bodies of Thai girls
and boys, flailing limbs of Australian surfers
and German stutterers, British bushwhackers

and French speculators. No sooner does Justice
slide on the dance floor than he comes face
to face with Salome, disco queen adorned

this night in lamé halter and silver rings.
It's love at first sight, she's been waiting
for Justice all her nights, dancing meanwhile

in platform shoes and high slit skirt. This night she
dances only with him through the hours, she clings to him
like destiny, accepts his kind offers of drinks

and company. She's slender and smooth and silky
and Justice forgets his disappointment in her
glow. Amid veils of light and damp odor of part-

recognized lust, he dances around her
and the edge of her sleeves flutters, strokes him
like unfinished sunlight and again

he's a bit dazzled, a bit giddy feeling
good to be here, feeling some knot loosening,
letting go of whatever else he's been bound to

all these years. Babylon's too far away
and lechery is undoing his habits. Now

he's almost ready to let it all go when
hazy with glee he totters out on the beach
and under moonlight, he turns to her with half

a mind to move closer, but outside the walls
of Green Mango, Salome seems a tad more
sinister in a way Justice can't put his finger

on, and he doesn't. There is a shadow where
a shadow shouldn't be – a hair out of place,
some hint that a light's gone murky,

the thought a tad filmy, something awry.
Suspicion that Salome is not

the kind of girl he's used to eats through him
like a bad sermon, the stars too bouncing in
the darkness like demons mocking his fear...

So what has opened closes over him, what
existed for a moment now moves to push
the space between Justice and temptation,

the gap now widens and he's back on one side
looking over the distance at her, long hair
loose in the night. In the cab, she leans over him

as they travel the short road home, and he slides
away, not touching and making a move,
paralyzed with no desire but to flee

this captivity. Half a mind wondering
if she's paid for at this point, the other half
seeing the thing in between, knowing the divide

and fearing that knowledge. Hair raising
alarm grows too loud for Justice
and he hurls himself out of the car, running

from the mystery he doesn't want to solve.
Behind him, Salome's angry now and calls
to him, curses him in Thai and maybe it's Justice's

imagination, but where he's hiding from,
her voice goes a pinch deep and gives him
reason to leap over the dune grass towards

the lights of home. Panic rises in the American
enforcer as he creeps around the tangles and vines,
shrubs and brushes, backslides across ivy walls

with arms out, head swiveling left to right
until he gets to the beach, and he crouches low
there, near the palms and avoiding the open sea

and the lights. Back in Brooklyn, he's prosecuted
countless transvestite girly-men who hid razors
in their Wonder Bras and strangled enemies with

Victoria's Secret thongs. He would have figured it
out sooner if only he were back in America. Now,
he can't even tell from a foot away what he's looking at.

He's without motion, watching the strange night
air as if he could see something, and know
for sure but all is still, he waits, watching

the tree tops move to slight wind, and somewhere
in his memory he sees the question:
What is he meant to see? Who is that girl

in his orbit for all these hours? Now, he allows
himself the thought of her as a boy. Safe, he allows
that mystery to slide into a mean longing, lets

it flicker while he blinks, then draws
himself up, the string taut around him, harder
now that he sees the danger in the easing

of the soul around things of this nature. He
can lie back like any man and enjoy his margaritas
in a sauna, but he can't forgive these episodes

that test his rectitude and try his soul. As he jogs
along the shoreline in the coming dawn, he knows
this to be a narrow escape from chaos and shame

and he wears that certainty now inside his skin,
plants it in himself like a seed so his blood
would feed on it and even his pulse would know

it and beat its knowledge in him forever.
He tries to unthink the possibilities
of revelation, stick to the plan

in vanquishing sin, and in this realm
of transgression, Justice prevails.

XIX. Dengue Fever

What with the transvestite chasing down
Justice and Jon Farang lost to chatter
and the Island, we are now formally disgruntled.

Eden is not what it's cracked up
to be. Maybe our good karma's gone bad
and there's a little hell in paradise; the next

day on the way down from the hills we run out
of gas and Baby J. throws out his shoulder pushing
the motorbike and has to exchange his sunglasses

for the local gas station attendant cum medic
to wheel his bone back in its socket. Later,
I burn the skin off my leg dismounting

the same bike at a natural tourist attraction
of waterfall and cave related fauna.
Our welcome worn out, it seems, Samui's

gods are sick of us and want us out of there.
It's clear that Jon Farang has been taken
and will not be returned to us, the man without

earthly possessions stays while we three must go.
"Suppose we take a boat to Ko Pa Nga for a day
or two," I say that night as Justice rubs up

against the rubber whale on the surf like Burt
Lancaster against Deborah Kerr. The lusty
little monkey's missing his girl something hard

and it'd only do him good to go. Next morning,
we taxi across to the other side and board the boat
to Haat Rin Beach and come face to face with three

American girls reclining on deck.
The middle one listens to her walkman
while another looks back towards Samui. The short

hair blond stares past us with haunted eyes
and we get the feeling we're going the wrong way.
She moves feebly from the mast, and Justice steps

up to her side. She talks above a mere whisper
hollowed out and layered in burnt cells
and marrow. In her voice we hear bones breaking,

skin rotting in sores, timbre that once might have
graced the world with song now a shadow cracking
in salt and sun. She's been bitten, blood

poisoned by the dengue mosquito, and she
lay delirious on her cot for ten days straight
while the fever took a hammer to her bones

and shattered the sternum, the clavicle,
the scapula, the humerus, the ulna,
their radius, the metacarpus, even

the bones of her fingers and her pelvic girdle.
The femur and patella were not spared.
It crushed her fibula and tibia and the seven

bones of her tarsus so that she can't stand
and when the fever left, her skeleton quiet,
the poison fed on her skin, another week

when the itch of sores covered her head to toe.
At this point of telling she warns Justice
to be careful on Ko Pa Nga, the demon insect

comes not in evening but in day, its black
and white pattern like yin and yang is the stamp
of doom. She moves with a body fragile

from a test of fire, cleansed from useless
passions and sloppy wants, this body moves
out in clarity, still sick but getting better,

struggling to get back to the world, to reclaim
its flesh and muscle before her plague while
we stand rooted by fear and ruing our bad luck

that we are headed toward certain disaster.
Justice and I huddle against the tender breeze
while Baby mocks us for our terror. Our pale

messenger sits back by the two girls
and closes her eyes, missive delivered, warning
sounded, job done. The other two smile and laze

in the sun. Who knew we would be hunted this way
and who do we pray to? I see myself plunging
into the sea, yelling "save yourselves!" to Baby Jesus

and Justice before I hit the water and drown.
"Too late, too late now." I hear the trinity
chanting. "Too far to go back." Surely, Baby Jesus

suggests, that my drama's gotten away from me
and there's really nothing to fear. Maybe it's
our working class minds, or our Irish/Chinese

fatality, but Justice and I won't be
convinced of our immunity from affliction
because our genetic memory tells

a different story. We both know what begins
leads to the end at the end, and the start
is the same all over. The two bleed forever

into each other until they separate
again. That's the way of destiny
and we're heading towards the fever.

How lucky Farang is now basking
knee deep in the Gulf's salty spray, light laughter
chiming among tipsy shadows, wine and smoke

drifting from the Island's balcony, one Jew saved,
three Catholics set adrift in the dengue sea
and it's always too late to go back anywhere.

XX. Another Country

The day's already gone by the time our boat docks
in the marina and we disbarge onto the sand.
We head for Tommy's Restaurant though

we feel the closing sting of the mosquito
and sense the hard grind of murder everywhere,
killer insects hiding between paper napkins,

in the drain, the sewer, the wooden slats
of Paradise Bungalows which I keep
knocking on for luck and to chase the red ants

off the mosquito netted bed. Baby J. comes back
from the communal wash basin and reports
that he saw it flying around. "Well," I say,

"I'm just not going there. If it wants me, it's
gonna have to hunt me down. We'll see who gets
it first." In my adopted borough of Brooklyn

I defy death daily by evading communion
with lepers, vampires, ghouls, priests and actors,
so now I do the same with the dengue, ace

bone crusher. What could it do that killers
in Brooklyn can't? Masters of paranoia
and suspicion, certain we're within range

of the head dengue's radar, Justice
and I walk in half circles, tuning in to every
breeze and small tremors in the air, waiting

to be scanned down and sucked up, maybe
swarms will pull around us like a curtain
and leave us with nothing but chewed skin

on bones, or we'll be a happy meal for one,
then all of Justice's weight lifting and Mr. America
attitude will deflate like his bulges and swells.

But we go undetected and next day taxi
into the dengue territory of That Salan
over unpaved road, thrown around by

errant rocks and sand locked curves. No Samui,
this terrain's rocky, dry, no warm sand
or blue sky. Here's a place you can hide

from the oracle that predicts your part
in the world's final destruction. Here's the place
before anything ever happens, cloudy and mean

like Valhalla for the wrecks and pessimists, jungle
vines loop around branches like nooses, smell
of oblivion everywhere. We come

to the Island View Bungalows on a pebbly beach,
set our coils, light our incense like the room's
a shrine to repel the blood suckers' grip of pestilence.

Behind the bungalows — shanties and stray dogs
lead out to the jungle and a mythical waterfall.
We've heard from friends that "Ko Pa Nga's better

than the others." Now stupefied by fear I can't
see that truth and can only sit over the coils
facing the sea, picture wild uncharted plant

life and safe beasts like geckos and mountain turtles.
"It's paradise," friend Nava said. So is this it?
Where're the birds of paradise, the starry orbs?

Diaphanous seraphim and winged doves?
Instead of scented apples and roses
we have here the musk of clam shells

and mildewed abalone husks; instead
of holy dazzle we have the gray flat line
of horizon tearing across the water. Surely,

paradise is somewhere else where kids
are not ragged and dogs have a purpose.
And where's the Great Beauty to show us the way?

Nothing here but seafood noodle and Singha beer,
cigarettes, then sleep and more noodles and beer.
Nothing here but dengue threat and dregs of the sea.

"It's paradise," she said. But its gates are closed
and we can't afford the price of admission.
Not enough faith, love, charity, compassion.

On the island's edge we wait as the clear
water curves over cliffs and crashes down
on the rocks below, bulbous sego lilies shake

in the soil, hidden among unnamed Paleozoic
leaves opening their lips to the rushing water
and under the cloud scarred sky I think I hear

someone singing "hosanna" and see the falling
water, the lone lily under it, trapped against
the glistening rock, and the voice comes again,

"hosanna" and see the danger of the flower,
the roar, the inevitable falling
and the infinite threat sung again and

again. "hosanna, hosanna, hosanna."

XXI. Not Yet

It turns out I was dreaming of the flower
and it was Justice calling my name.

Nothing but food and slumber in the dark
afternoon, the mighty dengue looms over
minutes, hours, every moment monitored

by unseen evil and we're afraid of
every murmur in the damp air, each hum
sounds the song of doom. We hang around

the bungalow restaurant, drink whiskey,
eat, make friends with Mr. Tom, soon-to-be
teenage miscreant with a penchant for Jack Daniel,

and Brother Itt, Ray Ban wearing Marlboro
smoking sibling to Chan, wife of the absent
owner. Despite Itt's insubordinate slump

in the chair and disdainful attitude in
general, when we mention the King his hand
slides to where his heart would be and lets out

a moan of love. "I adore my King."
No doubt it's the only truth he believes.
Later that night, he takes us into a tent

behind the bungalows and introduces
a beer drinking ruffian Thai Rasta
and two more pot smoking home grown

hooligans. Itt's a hood too no doubt, but
we believe we're cared for and protected,
so we crawl on hands and knees through the flap

of the tent and sit cross legged in the circle
like pilgrims while the Rasta pulls out his pipe.
Milky smoke drifts, spreads like a shroud between

us, keeping the space uncertain. I lean
back to catch a glimpse of Baby Jesus, nervous
maybe, a little taut around the mouth, and I am

rudely spun free from the scene, jerked from this
moment into dimensions of air traffic
signals, rapid thundering flash of running

planes, hot blast of rockets going back against
our time, my limbs caught between crystal shards
and earth is the fortune teller's gear.

Fear of the fever's left me; I'm standing
on top of the waterfall watching
the hibiscus below, shaking at the force

of the deluge when a flash of light bursts
through the trees. I stand still. The wind starts too;
I hold up my hands to cover my face

but I let everything else go, alone.
I remember that fear I'm supposed
to have for death, that beauty dipped in gore.

But the light is not that. It's hands and faces
like maybe there're more than one idea, one life
hanging in the air there, so close to me that

the breath feels cool like a benediction,
unchained. From that light my paramour Baby
Jesus appears a part at a time, his palms out

and then fingers cut into them like edges
of a kaleidoscope, then his eyes, fragments
blur – it's no use to focus. Amber shards gleam

from his eyes, the gold so deep he looks
almost blind. Someone else is here too, another
hand brushes against my arm, lingers by

me while I, both mind and flesh still, rapt
and shot through with seeds of raging mercy.
And that's how I know who has come and what for:

All this is love I don't deserve, can't have, won't
get. This the promised land shown like bait to fish.
Here it is, it mocks me. *Here I am.*

I want to look away, but she's holding her
arm up, and once more the ferocity
charges through and electrifies my blood—

my memory short circuited by this kind
of compassion, a thing without delicacy,
without softened senses. The Goddess of Mercy

is for real and she's coming up behind me
now as Baby J. rises into sight again.
It's true then that this is paradise, the sphere

of love, luminous eternal empyrean
and I'm raging with it. Never would I know
its violence, its rowdy epiphany and stormy rapture

if I didn't feel it for myself.
Wait for me, I say to the Goddess
and Baby, *wait for me.* I kneel at the edge

of Nirvana for hours, days, weeks, years, eyes closed,
earnest, but it doesn't matter. When I
open my eyes again, the three of us are lying

face down on brown earth against dry grass,
Baby's hand in mine. Tent, Itt, hooligans
gone, heaven has vomited out we three

bad clams; we three crawl around the dirt a bit
and sit up in time to catch dawn breaking
on the water. Wild dogs bark up the road

as a whip of sunlight cuts through morning
and its fog. The gray shimmers a little
on its way out, and the world is exact again.

Again we are flesh. Under the cool wind
Baby Jesus reaches for me in human
love, us three each fallen, lost, abandoned.

And I lean back on him. *I shall be with you
always.* And we go and wait on the ocean wave.

XXII. Last Rites

And here is the answer: love and knowing
make us fly, wingless we make do with the cross,
bear it on our backs and soar, ride bareback

on heaven's splendiferous wave, rescue our own
festered sealed up souls from crypts and dungeons.
In our newfound wisdom, we see the errors

and beat the short retreat back to Samui,
we ride back on stormy tides to our lost
Farang, lavender evenings and merry twitter

among the camphor trees only to realize the cross
is heavy and we can't stay here forever. After
a meal of shark and tortellini we consult

The Lonely Planet and make our way south
via Phun Pin, a wretched stop-over town for tourists
on the way somewhere else. Farang's friend Mr. T

travels part way with us, and while a deranged
tourist videos the dirty menu, I order a fried rice
and Baby Jesus goes to rent a room upstairs

to store our luggage until our 3 am train. We walk
in the night market and pass stalls of nuts and bolts,
AA batteries and metal wires. Justice's looking to rid

himself of the three joints before we enter Malaysia,
where *dada** equals death. Meanwhile, I get a rumbling
in my belly where the fried rice should be,

and it dawns on me and runs through me that I've
ingested some vile thing, some sinister tentacle
that claws at my innards now. At midnight,

Mr. T leaves us and Justice wanders off looking
to shed his vice. I sit on a cane chair by the vermin
infested bed reading Conrad. He's just like me

writing in his second tongue — English more florid
than any American, each word bearing two worlds
crawling towards an end bearing two natures.

But this night, I'm too ill to live in either, to speak
in any tongue. Baby waits for Justice by the grimy
window while I step over the sleeping man across

our doorway and limp down the hall to
the shithole, and weak kneed I crouch
in the foul closet, I read the magic

marker warnings on the wall. *Dirty bastards!*
Someone's watching you, be careful. Watch
for the holes in the wall. In my fever and delirium

I see the holes at eye level and wonder who
would want to watch me now, bowels dug out
and putrid, pants around my knees holding

my breath so as not to let the stink in.
If anyone thinks this attractive, well, each
to his own smell. And what a smell it is as we

grow a little more alarmed at each foray
down the hall, each time a little worse until
I abandon all fear and lie atop the insects

and stinkbugs on the bed. Yet we are full
of fear as Baby holds my hand. He's nervous
for my life and for Justice, who has gone

into the night to abandon his sin.
In my delirium, I think I see him
smoking his joints one at a time in a bar.

He's eating very spicy food and applauding
the karaoke singer who just sang his heart
out under a grubby disco ball. He claps,

eyes watery in dope besotted conviviality,
taking it into his head that he has to egg
the singer on, that no one's appreciating

how hard he's trying. Then the murky dark
slides around, all visions now gone, I hear
Baby's soft breathing beside me and Justice

rattling the iron gate outside. He can't come
in and calls up until Baby finally hears him
and leaves me to find the gatekeeper's key.

To think, *dying in a hole like this, like drowning
in my own vomit.* The bugs are all over
me now, crawling on my earlobes, under

my fingernails, and I keep my eyes closed, preparing
for the final flutter, wings brushing against
my eyelids, and far away, a voice like my own

is saying, *come in. Come on in.* Then a voice not
my own says, *It's time to go.* The air gets thick
when I try to answer, but the voice not

my own cuts me off. *Are you ready?* Who's
saying that? But I'm ready. I open
my eyes. I hold out my hands. There's singing

somewhere, voice like a mountain boy
or sumptuous angel or both, again, I hear
hosanna, hosanna, soft soprano close to

my skin, and I'm weak with this brutal joy
that inflames my flesh faster than the fever.
Smashed with bliss I try to move

my tongue, to answer while pinned by thorny vines.
I am ready to crumble, dissolve, melt away
into this light if they would let me, but when it

drapes across the sky, I can't tell anymore
the time of day or night. All the world veiled
in one slow harmony, planets spin in drowsy laps

and moons crawl around their starry course, drunken
thieves caught by time and something else while the
hymns get louder. This time, it's not Justice calling

me but another, sweeter messenger
incanting the mantra, and I open my
arms to him, open my eyes to see his face,

sprawled on my back, set free to look at love, at Baby
Jesus calling my name,
hosanna, Joanna. And it's Baby
Jesus calling my name.

JOANNA SIT is the author of *My Last Century*. She was born in Canton, China but now lives in New York City.

SPUYTEN **D**UYVIL
Meeting Eyes Bindery
Triton
Lithic Scatter

Made in the USA
Charleston, SC
02 May 2014